LOVE
& SEX &
PORN

Jeromy Darling

DEDICATION

To my wife Gretchen. Neither of us pictured me doing this some day, or wading into this world. Thank you for loving me and being the exact kind of woman I would need to walk this road. To my sons, Wyatt, Wilder and Wren - you're all going to do bigger and better things than I ever will. I'm so honored to be raising boys in a time such as this. The world is going to need your courage. To my parents for showing me what marriage could be and rabidly supporting everything I do. To my siblings for standing on the wall with me. To Jenny Ochs and the ARC for giving me the chance to hone this message in front of thousands of kids.

And to those thousands of kids - I believe in you.

CONTENTS

ACKNOWLEDGEMENTS

I could not have written this book without the resources and tireless efforts of Fight the New Drug (fightthenewdrug. com), the National Center on Sexual Exploitation (ncose. com), The Abstinence Resource Center (www.arc.rocks), Professor John D. Foubert, and the great C.S. Lewis, who predicted this sexual anarchy back in 1952.

CHAPTER 1

Lies

I'm making a general assumption here that nobody reading this books lays in bed at night hoping and praying to have lots of bad sex throughout the course of their life. Instead, like most normal people, you lay awake in bed at night hoping and praying to have lots of good to great sex over the course of your adult life. I want that for you too. You deserve that, and I'm going to tell you how to get it. I'm not going to get into positions and techniques or anything like that, but I will tell you how to get it. I promise.

In order do this I need to dispel some myths and lies about sex. We are living in the most sex obsessed, sex saturated society that humanity has ever known. I call it sexual anarchy. My generation and the one coming up behind me is paying a very heavy price for this betrayal. (what betrayal?)

Let me explain.

If aliens came down today and landed in America (which is where they always land) and they decided that they were going to watch movies to learn about our species, they would get a grossly misrepresented view of what real sex is actually like between two people.

HOLLYWOOD'S LIES

Lie #1:

According to Hollywood, hot people always have great sex. Right? Whether it's a brief fling or a one night stand, if you get two hot people in bed it's instant chemistry, they know exactly what to do, they orgasm at the same time; it's like this perfectly choreographed dance (which by the way that's exactly what it is behind the camera). They go at it all night, they get up in the morning nobody has any gook in their eye or B.O. or morning breath, their hair is still perfectly in place and so is their makeup and this just must be what sex is like for all the beautiful people out there and their perfect lives. So you're left thinking one of two things to yourself: either you're thinking "well I'm a pretty good looking guy or girl so cool I'm just going to have great sex by default" or you're thinking "I'm not very good looking, I'm probably never going to be very good looking so shoot, I'm going to be relegated to the crumbs of sex for the rest of my lonely, pathetic life". I have good news for you (or bad news depending on how hot you think you are) your level of hotness, according to Hollywood's ever changing, and completely irrelevant standards has absolutely no bearing whatsoever over the quality of sex you're going to have over the course of your life. Their standards don't matter in the real world of sex. I promise.

Lie #2:

According to Hollywood If you've watched the "bromance" comedies or the "jock comedies", you know sometimes the tubby, likeable, not-so-attractive, pot-smoking loser, with a cool personality, can also bag a really hot chick if he tries hard enough, but it's never the other way around. When was the last time you saw a movie featuring a tubby, likeable not-so-attractive female character desperately trying to bag a really hot guy and then finally does? They don't make a lot of movies like that, right? I think Hollywood actually hates girls but that's another lecture for another day. Again, your level of hotness has no bearing over these things.

Lie #3:

According to Hollywood, to be great at sex, one needs to have sex with a lot of people, so that one can practice at sex and get better at it. If you believe that, let me state for the record: I pity the people you intend to practice on over the next five or ten years "getting better at sex". Sex is not like training for a marathon or the Olympics. You know how I know that? We've been having sex from the beginning of human history, like we've been eating, sleeping, pooping and walking around. We've also been busy copulating, pro-creating and repopulating the earth. Meaning: Instinctively, you have the ability to have sex with someone, know what goes where, and find some enjoyment in said activity, having never practiced. I would know that better than most people, but that story is a few chapters away. The only thing more sex with more people will make you great at is short-term relationships. Once a relationship becomes physical, It's all at least one person in that relationship (usually the guy) ever wants to do when you're together. A relationship like that will die a very quick, painful death when it becomes strictly physical.

CHAPTER 2

Love Defined

What do we need for a long lasting relationship? We need love, but what is love? Everybody throws that term around like we're all supposed to know what it means. It's as if people believe we all have the same definition of it, like we're gifted with an understanding of exactly what it is. But no one ever defines love in specific terms. Today, I'll define it for you; probably this will be the first and last time anyone's going to define love for you.

It's three things and if you miss even one you missed them all.

Love #1:

Love is forever. REAL LOVE is forever. I love my three

sons forever. I will never give them up for adoption if they bug me too much and move on with my life. I love my parents forever. Now not everybody can say that, I know that. Some people have really crappy parents. I spend a lot of time in my job trying to fix those kids. But I have great parents and I will never emancipate myself from them. I love my wife forever. "Oh but Jeromy, how can you know? That's different! What if some day you meet someone you're more attracted to, or someone you have better chemistry with, or you and your wife experience a conscious uncoupling, or you have irreconcilable differences?" And blahbity blah blah blah blah blah!!!"

Just relax ok?

Here are a few things I know about my future even though I can't predict it: I will never rob a bank no matter how broke I get (and I've been broke). I will never punch an old lady in the face no matter how angry I get (and I've been angry - I mean never at an old lady, but I've been angry). I know those things every bit as much as I know I will never leave my wife because I love her and love is forever. I promised by giving my word at my wedding in front of witnesses that I was never going to leave. If my sons can't trust me to keep the promise I made to their mother, who I'm regularly sleeping with, how in the world could they trust me not to eventually fall out of love with them some day, as well? They couldn't. They shouldn't. Deep down we know love is supposed to be forever and when it ends we know something is wrong.

Love #2:

Love is a choice. Believe it or not Gretchen actually chose to be with me. If you've seen pictures or videos of me online you'll understand how amazing this is. I didn't blackmail her or give her a love potion, she actually chose me and I chose her and in that choice, love can now blossom and grow. It cannot grow in a vacuum. Meaning you choose to love someone or not love someone based on all available evidence. So if there is force, pressure, deception, or coercion in the relationship - there cannot be love - because you have to be free to choose it.

Love #3:

Love at its core is a complete and total selfless act. Selfless is the opposite of selfish. It says someone else is more important than me. I change my son's poopy diapers every day, and not because it benefits me in any way to do so (believe me, when the poop gets under your fingernails because you're moving too fast trying to clean it up, you will reconsider why you do it every day). Yet there I am, every day, on my knees changing the diapers of two little boys in my house. I don't like how it smells. I certainly don't like looking at it, but I do it because they need me to. They can't do it themselves, and I'm their daddy, and someday I'll have to teach them how to use the restroom themselves.

Likewise, I try my best to put Gretchen's needs above my own. That doesn't mean she always gets what she wants; I don't always get what I want - that's not love. But at the end of the day, Gretchen's life, my sons' lives - they matter more than mine now. So if love at its core is a complete and total selfless act, is forever, and is a choice, I would argue so must sex be, and when you have two people in a committed, trusting marriage, who believe in love that lasts forever, giving each other choice and each trying to "out-selfless" the other person sexually - you have a recipe for mind-blowing sex every time.

There. That's the secret.

Whether it's five minutes or five hours, it will be mind-blowing.

...and I would argue you cannot get that level of trust and commitment in anything but a committed marriage where two people had the guts to stand up publicly and look each other in the eye and state "I will never leave you the matter how old or flabby you get". How do you intend on standing in front of another person completely naked AND unashamed without that commitment? I would argue that it's not possible. Shame, fear, doubt, and insecurity - those things ruin sex. Some of you reading this already know that. And those things tend to go away in a committed, trusting, forever-love marriage. If you think sex is there for you or for your orgasm or what you can take from someone else sexually, you're missing like 95% of what sex could actually be and I don't want that for you and I don't think you want that either.

CHAPTER 3

My 1st Time

Now is my favorite part of this little book because I get to tell you about my first time. You can relax. I've been told I should tone this part down a little bit so I will try and do that.

Gretchen and I got married on September 1st, 2002 at the US Bank Trust Center in downtown St. Paul. There were 400 people at our wedding, no kids and Gretchen had 12 brides-maids. Now if you've ever been to a wedding, and the bride has like, 5 or 6 bridesmaids, you're probably thinking "well she just has a lot of sisters". Gretchen has one sister and I have two. I've now run out of fingers to show how many women stood up for my wife that day, if that gives you any indication of the kind of woman I married. Somehow I managed to find 12 guys to stand up for me and it was an amazing day. We laughed and danced and ate and drank for hours. Now, I had been told by Hollywood that when that day finally came for this poor, miserable 21 year old virgin, there'd be only one thing that my little virgin brain would be capable of thinking about and all day long I'd be walking around like some kind of virgin zombie, completely unaware of any other reality other than the fact that after 21 years I was finally going to get laid. But then that day finally came and surprise surprise - that wasn't my experience at all. They were wrong again! I was present for my wedding. I have vivid memories of that day. I remember the people that came, the songs that were sung and the way she looked when she danced. I remember. I was there. In fact, we were the last people to leave the wedding. How's that for irony? We finally left and drove about a mile away to the Embassy Suites Hotel in downtown St Paul. What followed was, yes, to this day, one of the most amazing 45 minutes of my entire existence. We have since topped that night many times over the years. But for obvious reasons I will always keep that on my top ten list of sexual experiences. And every single joke and stereotype I've ever been told by Hollywood about how a 21 year old virgin's first time was supposed to go was nuked out of existence. They were wrong on every level. Think about what else they might be wrong in case you tend to take ALL your opinions from Hollywood stars. And you know what I wasn't thinking about that night? That first time? I wasn't thinking about all the other girls I'd been with. I wasn't closing my eyes, wishing Gretchen looked like that ex-girlfriend or would do the things that one girlfriend did. I didn't just give her my body, I gave her my memories. Oh, you didn't think about that did you? See, Hollywood wants you to think that there is no difference between your food appetite and your sex appetite. That what you have for breakfast is as inconsequential as who you sleep with that night, but sex is the most intimate act you can possibly perform on another person. It's the only act in the known universe which creates human life. That's why rape is such a heinous crime (in case you didn't know). You can't rape food you can't impregnate food, right? Those two appetites are very different. Every lover you collect along the way will be another ghost that haunts every future relationship. As you're trying to love the one you're with, you can't stop thinking about that old flame. Distracted sex is pretty miserable. I was not on some weird religious, fundamentalist mission, convinced that sex was dirty and should be done in the dark as quickly as possible - yet another stereotype I had to put up with from Hollywood. I simply felt the woman I claimed to love deserved no comparisons and for the rest of my life I'll never be picturing another woman when I'm having sex with my wife and nobody can take that from me... but by force.

CHAPTER 4

The Picture

I first met Gretchen in a picture on a wall. I was friends with her sister, Gena, and my sister and I went to Gena's apartment one day to hang out. Gena's room was covered in photographs, but there was one on the wall of Gretchen, a little bigger than the rest, that caught my eye. I remember thinking, very innocently, "that is the prettiest face I've ever seen in my life". I must have been gawking at it because Gena finally came over and was like "hey that's my sister".

I never thought I would meet Gretchen, but we did meet, a couple of weeks later, at church of all places. When I met Gretchen she was a hot mess. She spent all of high school drunk. From the age of 14 up to her senior year. In fact she drove drunk probably 15 or 20 times by her own volition.

That's literally one of the dumbest things you can ever do is drive drunk by the way. She's very lucky not to be dead or in prison.

She was not a virgin when I met her. She'd had a couple of boyfriends in high school. All she ever was to them was a body. She was raped at a party when she was 16. At 18 she finally hit a wall and realized a couple of things: 1. Alcohol had a death grip on her life. 2. She did not know how to have a functional relationship with a man that did not involve sex. And, frankly, alcohol and sex were exclusively combined in high school, so she could work up the courage for sex. Hey guys - a girl should not need to be drunk to get in the mood for sex. If she does need to be drunk something's very wrong. The irony is high school was very good to Gretchen. She was quite popular at a very large high school not because she wanted to be, or because she tried. Gretchen just IS. She's the most magnetic human being that I've ever met in my life. You could drop her in a remote village on the other side of the world and she'd come out Queen in a week. I don't know how she does it. I mean, I studied it, I'm a victim of it, heck - she doesn't even know she's doing it, but it did her no favors in high school. You know why? Because that kind of popularity never actually does what it's promised and it nearly ruined her.

I didn't know any of this the night that we met - we just shook hands and said "hello". We very quickly became best friends, which for me was a brand new experience. Growing up I never had a best friend. I barely had any friends. Other than my own mother, no one in my life to that point had been as kind to me as Gretchen and that fact was not lost on me. What I wanted growing up was what my parents had. I wanted to love a woman the way my dad loved my mom; it was the best thing he ever did for us. I recognize that that might sound crazy to some of you reading this because maybe your parents are divorced or they're miserable. If that's true, then today I will apologize on their behalf - I'm sorry. You deserved better than that from them. I don't know what their issues are, but their marriage does not have to dictate yours. If anything they showed you what not to do, which is not much I recognize, but it's something. I wanted what my parents had so I decided I would wait until I met a girl that could put up with me for like 80 years. That's a lot to ask somebody - "give me the rest of your life". You are not that special or interesting that somebody should agree to do that. By the end of the summer I knew what was happening and so did my dad. One day he asked me if I could live without her, "because if you can you should" he said. And I knew the answer right away. "No. If she moved away or she fell in love with someone else I would never recover. I'd be chasing her or someone like her for the rest of my life." She'd set the bar too high and I didn't want to live like that. So I took her for a walk and I told her to her face "I don't want to do this with anybody else.

I'd like to marry you someday. If you're not interested in that you should let me know, but I needed you to know... and she did feel the same.

Then, about a year before we got married, I worked with this guy. He was baffled that we were saving ourselves. "Why would anybody do that?" he asked. So I told him, "I don't know any other way to show a woman that I'm serious about her than to withhold that act which creates human life until I put a ring on her finger and promised in front of witnesses that I was never going to leave. Having sex with her is not going to do that, that's what her boyfriends did - they used her and I'm never going to be that guy".

I've spent 18 years trying to reprogram her brain from just what four years of high school taught her about love and body image, but because of the decision she made at 18 to not have sex, even with me, until we were married 3 1/2 years later, she was also able to come to our bed the night of our wedding, fully trusting I was a man of my word and not comparing me to the boyfriends she'd had in high school. Not like that would have been that much to live up to, high school sex is not all that great - some of you already know that, but I can't tell you how hard it's going to be for you to do what she did if you don't start right now in your youth, ok?

CHAPTER 5

The Numbers

Now it's story time. I'm going to read you some stats. Why? Because numbers don't lie. Actually, they tell a story, so I've got a story. 1 in 2 American adults will get an S.T.D. at some point in their life. Any math whiz out there want to tell me what the percentage is on 1 in 2? 50%. Little life tip: 50/50 odds, NOT in your favor when it comes to your physical well being and your genitals should never be taken. I can't believe I even have to write that. If you're standing on the ledge of a bridge and you're thinking of doing an extreme base jump into a river below and a mathematician happens to wander by and say, "oh, excuse me sir/ma'am but you know based on your height and weight and the rate of speed at which you hit the water and the rate that the rapids are moving there's about a 50/50 chance that you'll break both your legs if you don't hit the water at just the right angle". Not a single one of you reading this, with an 8th of a brain, would make that jump. You would step down onto the ground, hug the mathematician - heck you'd probably offer to buy him a drink to thank him for saving you from that indignity. Today you readers are the extreme base jumpers and I am the mathematician. Some day in the future if you've taken my advice and you're of legal age and you happen to see my wife and me out on a hot date (which is pretty much every Thursday night) and you want to buy me a drink to thank me for saving you from any one of these terrible diseases that I'm about to recite - I give you permission today to buy me a drink.

...lest you get something like, I don't know, HPV - the human papilloma virus (genital warts). This is a viral infection that infects six million new Americans every year. It can be transferred through any kind of sex you can have with someone including skin to skin contact and contact with body fluids - meaning you don't have to be having sex with someone to get HPV In fact many scientists believe it's so common now that close to every sexually active person is probably just walking around with it and doesn't realize it yet. Some don't get symptoms with HPV some get warts on their genitals and it can cause cervical cancer depending on the strain. Hey fellas, I don't know if you know this but you don't have a cervix. Ladies you do and you do not want cervical cancer. There is no cure for HPV. If often goes away on it's own after a few years, depending on the strain. The warts can be treated, but they will come back. Condoms curiously have no reduction or prevention whatsoever against HPV and this is the most common viral S.T.D. you can get. Wait what? That's right - you've been lied to again. "Oh if you're going to have sex, use protection, be safe. Safe? Safe from what? According to the C.D.C. (the Center for Disease Control) the most common viral S.T.D. is impervious to condoms - and has no cure. Neither does herpes by the way, which is the second most common viral S.T.D. Has anybody ever told you that? That's what I thought.

How about chlamydia? This is a bacterial infection that infects one to three million new Americans every year and can be transferred any kind of sex you can have with someone. Meaning unless you plan on wearing a condom over your mouth you can get chlamydia (and pretty much EVERY OTHER S.T.D) orally and anally. In fact most STDs can also be transferred to a baby - that had no choice but to be born inside a diseased body. Sorry back to chlamydia. Some don't get symptoms, but if you do they made include pain when going to the bathroom or discharge coming from the penis or vagina. Discharge is a smelly, yellow fluid that sort of drips out of you all day and there are millions of folks today just walking around trying to figure out how they're going to hide that drip from their friends and family all day, until they're in so much pain they finally go to a doctor, only to realize they waited too long and now they've developed pelvic inflammatory disease - that's when the blood starts coming out. Good news is condoms might actually have some reduction here - assuming you're going to wear one over your mouth or just not use your mouth during sex (which I wouldn't recommend). This is still the most common bacterial STD you can get and women acquire this more easily than men. In fact women tend to acquire STDs more easily overall. Do you know why? Because usually there's something left inside her when he's done.

Chlamydia does have a cousin too, called gonorrhea - the second most common bacterial S.T.D. There are two of these diseases coming after you and now they found strains of super chlamydia and super gonorrhea and super syphilis. Do you know why they call them super? Because they've grown resistant to every known drug. So let's do the math: human beings have sex with multiple partners throughout the ages, eventually develop STDs, then eons later scientists finally come along to develop drugs to combat the STDs but only succeed in making some of them stronger. Isn't that interesting? I mean one could hypothesize that if tomorrow every person on earth woke up tomorrow and decided to be monogamous (that's one partner for life) eventually STDs would be eradicated from the face of the earth right? I mean at some point right? So whether you believe in God or evolution or nature, it's pretty clear that there is something inside our bodies that prefers it to be monogamous. Otherwise how would you even get an STD? Where did they even come from? There are 26 known STDs on the face of the earth, and since you've never seen a movie or a T.V. show featuring a recurring character with an STD (because apparently in Hollywood no one ever gets them), I now have to tell you what happens when you get one - are you ready? You have to tell the next person that you're going to have sex with that you're infected. Do you think they're going to have sex with you then? That's why most people just don't tell right? And then you meet the person that you want to spend the rest of your life with but you have HPV, do you know what that means? That person has to choose to contract your disease and maybe spend the rest of their life with it in order to be with you. Or they could choose to just not be with you at all. 6 million people every year have to make that decision - what is worth? Sex? Orgasm? Do you know the average length of time two people spend having sex today in America? 3 minutes. 3 minutes to be exposed to twenty six known STDs. I hope you're smarter than that.

I have more numbers here, culled by very smart people whose names I can't pronounce and they went around asking people about their sex lives and got some very interesting data.

L I V I N G   T O G E T H E R

Seems pretty logical right? Here's the key to my apartment let's take the next step in our relationship and get some practice at this marriage thing. Except affairs happen twice as often with individuals that are living together than those that are married meaning the moment you move in with someone, you just doubled the chances one of you is going to cheat. Couples the do live together until marriage are still less sexually faithful after marriage than those that did not live together first. Out of all the people that live together 70% of live-ins will never even get married, meaning you're more likely never to get married than get divorced if you move in with someone. Couples that do manage to make it to marriage have a 50% higher rate of divorce than couples that did not live together first. I call that sabotage. For most people, living together is relationship sabotage. Apparently there's just something about putting a ring on a finger and making a promise at some kind of matrimonial ceremony - which every single civilization ever known to mankind has done - that actually makes a person more likely to stick around and be faithful. Look at that - we just learned something about ourselves from human history. Did you even know that was possible? I mean one could almost surmise that we're preprogramed in our genetic code with a desperate need for a lifetime companion. you even see it among the animal kingdom. You can also see it inside our bodies as they reject multiple partners with STDs. I think that's very fascinating no? Just me?

C O N D O M S

How about condoms? Consistent and correct condom use is not common. Not even half of teenage boys use one consistently. Approximately 15% of girls that depend on condoms to not get pregnant will still get pregnant within a year. If a sexually active 15 year old girl practices a typical use of condoms she has a 50% chance of getting pregnant by the time she's 20 and 80% of teenage fathers will leave after putting a baby inside a girl. Sorry ladies, I guess those are the kind of men were raising today. Just trying to keep you off the ledge remember? Please don't hate me. I didn't make the numbers up.

M A R R I A G E

Put your parents' marriage aside for a second ok? Married people have significantly higher levels of happiness than people that are not married, they fight less, they make more money. Ooooh this is interesting - marriage provides the highest levels of sexual pleasure and satisfaction for men and women, and that study has the most studies of all the studies on my list of studies. "Wait Jeromy, weren't you saying something like that earlier?" Why yes observant reader I was! "You mean to tell me that two people in a committed trusting marriage, regardless of their levels of hotness according to Hollywood, actually have better sex and more frequent orgasms than your average sexy twenty-something single living in up in New York City like I see on all my favorite shows"? That's exactly what I've been saying this entire time and now my numbers back it up over and over and over again. "But Jeromy, the divorce rate is 50/50. You just told us not to take those odds"! You're right. I did. You got me. I'm so embarrassed. Hey is that marriages fault though? Is that why the divorce rate is so high? Are we the first civilization ever to finally discover that marriage is unnecessary and deeply flawed and not needed for a thriving society? Is that why the divorce rate is 50/50? 90% of you reading this (if you're not married yet) will be married by the time you're 30, regardless of how high that number climbs and while you are married, briefly, you're suddenly having better sex than you were when you were single. So I've got a theory: I think we're so sexually broken in the age of sexual anarchy the not even marriage can fix us anymore and I don't want that for you and that's why I'm writing this to you.

PREGNANCY

Surely there is some good news here? Sadly, no. A sexually active teenager who does not use contraceptives has a

90% chance of getting pregnant within one year. I mean that seems pretty logical right? That's sort of the biological reason for sex. Approximately one million teen girls in America get pregnant every year, the highest of all industrialized countries on Earth and one in seven sexually active 14 year old girls becomes pregnant, in spite of all our education. I know what you're thinking though: "Well Jeromy if I get pregnant I can just have an abortion!" That's true. It's it's legal to do so. It's your body. I'm just telling you that by the time you find out you're pregnant, which is, oh, 4 or 5 weeks later when you've missed your period, there's already a little heartbeat inside you that started about 16 to 21 days. I don't have to be a girl to know it's going to be a lot harder to pull the trigger on an abortion when there's a beating heart right? Oh the irony that a heart would start beating a week before you even know it's there. That's all I'm saying ok?

BAGGAGE

I don't have numbers on shame/regret/guilt/baggage, but I can tell you this: it's been 18 years since Gretchen has been with any boy but me. That's half of her life. She still has bad dreams to this day about friends. Anyone want to explain that one to me? We ran into an ex once - on a date. He was the server at our table. I thought it was pretty funny until I looked at her face. The the most confident, well spoken woman I have ever met was stuttering, stammering, red-faced, with tears in her eyes - and he wasn't even that bad of a guy. I'd like to never see that look on her face again. Somebody want to explain that one to me?

CHAPTER 6

Porn

Now we're going to talk about porn. Nothing will affect your sexuality today more than your relationship with pornography. And I know what you might be thinking by this point. "Man this is like the greatest sex talk ever. I'm totally going to save myself for marriage, but what do I do in the meantime with all of my sexual energy? Oh I know! I'll just watch porn! It'll be me and porn until I get married! I can do this abstinence thing!"

In the the 1970s, if you wanted to see a porno, you had to be 21, drive to a movie theater in the seedy part of town, display a valid ID, purchase a ticket, and sit in the movie theater WITH OTHER PEOPLE, watching what are now NC-17 rated movies on Netflix. Try touching yourself in that environment guys. Then the 80s came around and now if you were under 21 you had some options: you could steal a magazine from a gas station or swipe your parents' credit card and order a VHS tape from a catalog (remember those?). However, you most definitely would get caught. Then the 90s came around. I remember the 90s. I was coming of age in the 90s. Grunge rock and forgettable pop-rock bands filled the airwaves. Then some guy named Tim invents the World Wide Web and suddenly you could just sit at the computer, login into AOL and type in "boobs" and "sex" and all kinds of crazy pictures would come up - albeit very slowly on the 56k modem dial up speed that we had back then. Now here we are today: every industrialized country on earth has mobile, streaming, 4G, broadband Internet and every person reading this book has a smartphone where you can speak to an artificial intelligence and have it pull a thought from the air and display it in front of your face in a couple of seconds. Completely free, unfettered, 24/7 access to hardcore pornography in the pockets of every child in America. What could possibly go wrong?

Do you know the average age of exposure to pornography today is between 8 and 11 years old? Some you are probably thinking "Oh yeah, that's that's when I first saw it. Yikes! My brother showed me or my friend." You know the most avid viewers and consumers of pornography? "College guys!" Nope. "Dirty old men?" Nope. 12 to 17 year olds. They're watching more porn than anybody else. It's our new sex education. Do you know what two of the most popular forms of pornography are online today? Teen and rape. Those are two of the most sought out forms of pornography online today. In fact a recent study showed that 88% of porn produced today features violence against women and 95% of the time when a woman is abused during a sex act she pretends to enjoy it and begs for more. So ladies let me just ask: what do you think happens to girls in a society where you're growing up around boys that are watching that kind of porn every day for ten years? We're finding out right now aren't we? Just one of the popular "tube" websites (because I know nobody reading this is paying for porn - you're watching the free stuff on pornhub or redtube or youporn or xvideo or xhamster), just one of those sites averages 6,000 streaming videos per second - from just one website. In 1998 there were 14 million pornographic web pages. Today there's almost 3 billion. Did you ever wonder where all of the free porn comes from? I mean that's a lot of porn right? Who's making all of this? Ever thought about that? Do you think that girls just turn 18 and wake up so horny (even though they're nowhere near their sexual peak), that they want to have violent sex with some guy, put it online for the whole world to see, but no one's going to give them any money or know their name or maybe even see their face? Have you ever met a girl like that? A good portion of the free porn is pirated from the "professional websites", but what about the other millions of videos? I now have to tell you where they come from - your messenger of death - and we'll see if you want to watch porn after that.

S L A V E R Y

Here in America, the land of the free the home of the brave, where slavery has been outlawed for hundreds of years, we spend more money buying underage boys and girls for sex in human trafficking than we spend on sports. It's a multibillion dollar industry - sex slavery. Slavery brings in more money today than it ever has in the history of our country. One child sold a minute. The average age that a girl is trafficked is 12 years old and once a pimp has sufficiently broken her body in (which is the first thing he does) she will work 20 to 50 men per day in a revolving door, on a mattress on the ground, until the sweet release of death at the ripe old age of 32 years old. That's the average lifespan for a victim of human trafficking before they die of disease or drugs or suicide. You know what we found out when we talked to some of these victims around the country - the few that we can even find? All of their stories were the same: every day their pimp or the cowards that bought them, brought their phones and filmed them. Regularly. Then they put those videos up on pornhub and redtube and youporn and the like, to make money off of the ad revenue. That's how those free sites stay alive you know - the ad revenue. You know what that means right? Every guy reading this, and probably some of you girls, have seen a video featuring an underage sex trafficking victim and you didn't even know it...but you enjoyed it right? "Well that's not fair, I didn't know! I don't want to watch that stuff"! Well good for you. I'm glad we've established that. But now what? Next time you pull up one of those porn videos, you're going to remember what I said here, so what's your plan? Are you gonna look really close and try to figure out if she actually looks 18? Are you gonna look really close and try to figure out if she looks like she's actually enjoying it? Or if it looks like it's professionally done? A good pimp can make a $1,000/hr off of ONE GIRL. You don't think they have money for nice cameras and lighting? Or a camera crew? You think pimps adhere to the terms and conditions on the websites before uploading? They have to agree that every performer in the video was 18 and gave their consent to be in the video. Kinda like how you agreed you were 21 when you entered the website right? Ok ok, I know guys that girls are complicated creatures. They're different from us. I've lived with one for many years - they take work. Porn doesn't take any work. I mean God forbid you ever work for something in your life. What good could possibly come from hard work?

Look, I realize society speaks out of both sides mouth to boys. On one side girls say "looks don't really matter", but when we go to YouTube all we see is Bieber in his underwear or Zac Efron in his underwear or any number of the One Direction boys in their underwear, behaving badly and girls go nuts for it so "what do they even want?" you say to yourself. "You know what I don't even care. It's too much work. I'm just going to watch porn and play video games and live in my parents' basement. It's not so bad". That would be a funny joke, but the joke's on us because it's happening all over this country. Young men are abandoning relationships altogether for porn and their hand, at numbers we are woefully ill-prepared to deal with. In fact Japan is experiencing this first hand. They're showing us our future. Their population sits at 186 million but in 46 years, before I'm dead, they will lose a third of their population down to 87 million. Do you know why? They are so over-porn'd and over-sex'd and over-tech'd in that country that their young people have stopped having sex altogether. No marriage. No boyfriends and girlfriends. No dating. No hooking up. They just stopped procreating. If that doesn't change, my great grandchildren will likely live in a world with there are no Japanese people left. They will have gone the way of the Mayans. Sounds crazy right? Actually right now in Japan you can buy a little holographic girlfriend that sits inside of a lamp. You can put it next to your bed at night. She'll talk to you, kiss you goodnight, be your alarm clock in the mornring, geez she'll even text you when you're gone "I miss u", "come home soon", "hows ur day?". So you know what Japan is doing? They're building sex robots. That'll fix the problem right? And ladies I hate to break it to you but they're not building a lot of male sex robots. They're mostly female sex robots with perfect bodies that won't cry or say no or feel any pain. So what happens to girls in that society? We're about to find out. That's the future we've been handed. So how did we get here? I mean how do you go from pretty vanilla porn in the 70s to rape porn just 40 years later? And speaking of which, where do you go after rape porn? What is next? You think it's just going to stop there?

S C I E N C E

So there's a science behind all of this. I bet you didn't think this abstinence nut was pro science, but I am. I love science. Now we have decades of research from brain doctors and neuropsychologists all over the world that have combined their data and do you know what they found? Your Brain on porn looks just like your brain on crack cocaine. **It does the same thing to your brain.** We're rewiring the neurons of an entire generation of children, **when their brains are most plastic**, to prefer violent digital sex over the real thing.

Here's how it works in layman terms: little Tommy gets his hands on some porn at 8 years old, maybe a brother or a friend showed him. He will never forget that picture as long as he lives (you're thinking of the first porn you saw right now aren't you?) and at 11 or 12 when he goes through puberty he's going to go back to that picture and in that wonderful moment his brain will produce a chemical called dopamine and drip it into the middle of the feel-good center of his brain, the amygdala (pronounced uh-mig-duh-luh), and his little body will start to shake as he gets an erection. You guys reading this out there are probably recognizing this experience now huh? Tommy's never felt this before. So he goes back the next day and the next day all the while making sure that no one ever sees what he's doing, because even though no one told him porn was wrong he's terrified about what's happening inside of him. This goes on for a while until one day, the shakes go away and so does his erection. You know why? His brain has already created new neural pathways and now, like a drug addict, he needs a stronger hit to get his fix. So Tommy goes on to one of those "tube" sites and starts clicking around on real categories like "Extreme Brutal Gang Bang", "18 and Abused" or here's one "Girls Crying" - that's a REAL category, on dozens of websites, with millions of videos featuring girls sobbing while someone does something to them. How do you think those videos got made?

Now Tommy never thought he'd be looking at this stuff. But in that wonderful moment his brain is now alive again, dripping more dopamine than it ever has and the shakes are back and so is his erection. Finally he's got a new fix! Just like a drug addict. This goes on for another couple of years until he finally gets in bed with a real girl only to find out in that one terrible moment that that's not what girls like in real life and she runs screaming out of the room "Assault! Assault!" But he's thinking to himself "She said yes! She gave consent! I thought that's what girls like"! This is assuming that he can even get an erection in that moment because his brain, which controls his penis, might not even know what's going on after all the porn it's been exposed to. So he goes to the doctor and says "Hey doctor, I'm 19, I'm pretty healthy, but I was trying to have sex with my girlfriend and I couldn't get an erection. I think I have erectile disfunction". And the doctor says "Um, can I ask you some questions?" and Tommy says "Well yeah sure". So the doctor says "Well you seem pretty young to have erectile dysfunction. Do you watch porn?" And Tommy says "Yeah of course I watch porn!" And the doctor says "Ok, can you get an erection when you watch porn?" And Tommy sneers "Of course I can get an erection when I watch porn!" So the doctors says "Well then you don't have erectile dysfunction Tommy. You have something else and I don't have a pill for that." 26% percent of men today, UNDER 40 years old, have erectile dysfunction. 1 in 4. 40 years ago that number didn't even exist, meaning it's going to keep climbing higher and higher until it's consumed every guy who thinks he can have a recreational relationship with pornography. So now Tommy has one choice left: he'll do what hundreds of thousands of cowards do every day - he'll go online to Backpage or Craigslist or maybe a more fancy looking website, hunting for an escort, no a prostitute, no... an under-age sex trafficking victim, that he can buy to pay to let him do what his girlfriend won't. In fact he'll even bring his phone in and pull up his favorite porn video and show that girl exactly what he wants to do to her. Just when you thought those girls' lives could get any worse. See the connection? Porn is creating a generation of sexually dysfunctional monsters that have to buy a girl to get what they've been watching and now slavery is exploding at numbers we've never seen.

So since I don't want that future for any guy reading this book - a broken penis or you turning into a villain that buys a human being for sex - can I just make one small tweak to your future? **Don't watch porn.** Save the world and don't watch porn. I know it sounds crazy right? Like how is that even possible? How can you even live without porn? What did the world do for centuries upon centuries before all of this porn? Actually we did a lot of cool stuff: we defeated Nazis and built rockets. There's a lot of great things you can do with all of that free time on your hands - no pun intended. I have TWO filters on my phone, two on my home WiFi. I have set parental controls on every Internet enabled device in my house. I even blocked Google, Bing and Yahoo from my house. I don't trust their safe search as far as I can spit. I don't care if you think I'm crazy. I am done being a guinea pig for a $100 billion a year global failed experiment on children. That's how much money porn brings in around the world. That's more than Apple, Google, Yahoo, Netflix, and Microsoft combined. Worse yet - 85% of that porn is produced by one company: **MindGeek**. Google them. They make big tobacco look like the Apostle Paul. I want them out of my life, I want them out of my boy's life and I want them out of my wife's life. Girls do you have a plan yet to compete with porn? Because you're going to need one. My wife has had 3 C-sections. THREE. In case you don't know what a C-section is I'll tell you: they cut you open about 4 inches below your belly button. Then they stretch that wound and put clamps in to keep it open. Then they take your intestines and put them on a tray. Then they take a little flexible tube and wrap it around the baby, cut the womb open, pull the baby out, close the womb, pull the tube out, put your intestines back inside you, take the clamps out, stretch the skin back shut, sow you up and then sometimes they staple the wound for good measure. My wife's had that done 3 times to bear my children because she has a very rare condition where she'll die if she gives birth naturally. You don't think her body has changed just a little bit since she was 18 or 19? I like it better now. She doesn't believe me but I do. Only because I worked to keep Gretchen, **and not porn**, at the sexual forefront of my imagination. I'm not heterosexual. I'm not homosexual. I'm not pansexual or A-sexual, or bisexual. **I'm gretchensexual**. I'm not literally attracted to half the population. It's just her. I think she's earned that no? Having her body ripped open, risking her life to bear my children. I think a small token of my appreciation for that would be to give her my sexuality for the rest of my life no? So that's exactly what I've done.

GIRLS

Girls I will be the last guy to ever tell you this: you don't have to look, act, or have sex like a porn star. If you think you do you will learn to hate sex. It's no secret that young girls around this country, in high school or college, find sex to be not very pleasurable, painful in fact, and really "more for a guy". I don't care what you believe - if a whole generation of girls doesn't think that sex is pleasurable what do you think is going to happen to us?

If you're with a guy that thinks there's nothing wrong with porn you should break up with him. Because he doesn't think you're human. That's what porn is designed to do - **to dehumanize** you down to an object. That's what his brain is seeing thanks to porn - the object center in his brain lights up and you're no longer a person. You can't compete with that.

If you're with a guy that asks you to text him or Snapchat him some nudes you should break up with him because he's a coward. He would never pull you aside privately and say "Hey quick, no one's looking, take all your clothes off and let me stare at you for five minutes - I won't touch you". What exactly is the difference there? I mean if an old man asks a teenage girl for a naked photo and a young man asks teenage girl for a naked photo what exactly is the difference? According to US laws you've now just produced or dissemi-nated or viewed child porn. All federal crimes. And we have normalized this behavior in every middle schools and high schools around this country, in less than ten years! What's next? Listen, I've never met a girl that wants to be with a coward. Almost every girl (not all) wants to be loved by one man for the rest of her life. Every single love story from the beginning of time has revolved around that one single idea. So if that's you and you compromise that desire to be the little porn star that boys want you to be you will be licking the bottom of the barrel, splintering your tongue for one last taste of what was supposed to be love and I don't want that for you and that's why I wrote this book.

The pornification of America is complete friends. It's how we have twerking and Kardashians and Miley Cyrus and Nicki Minaj and Lady Gaga. Porn-influenced pop stars are competing for girls attention, with their surgically enhanced bodies, airbrushed on the cover of every magazine, working out 4 hours a day with LAs top trainers, eating perfectly proportioned organic foods, and then turning around and telling all the "normal girls", just like Lady Gaga did after Super Bowl 51, that "I love my body and you should too". See Hollywood speaks out both sides of it mouth to girls too. "All women's bodies are beautiful! You don't have to look like me! Let's celebrate women's bodies! All shapes and sizes! Here's a selfie of me not wearing any makeup - aren't I brave! I'm just like you!". They think girls are that stupid. They don't care about you. They would never go back to looking like you. They'd rather kill themselves. And you can never look like that without money and synthetics meaning **we have no idea anymore what it means to be beautiful** - it's been stolen from you. 20 years ago my wife was trying to be skinny skinny skinny because that's what was beautiful

20 years ago, but what is it today? 2017 it's thick and booty-licious, big boobs, big butts, Beyoncé, Kim Kardashian, and what's it going to be 20 years from now? You don't know, but you're going to chase it through time - like a dog chasing a car - never catching it, but trying so hard. I see it in all the sexy selfies that you post on Instagram late at night in front of the mirror. You put on some really tight outfit, posing and preening and pouting for hours. Then you use all those special apps to wipe away the things you don't like, find some inspirational quote online (because you can't come up with one yourself) and then you post it with some emojis hoping you get enough likes that night from your friends and the strangers that have followed you (thanks to your clever use of hashtags) that maybe you'll feel like a celebrity that night, but then you wake up in the morning and you look in the mirror and you're stunned when you find that you still hate the shape of your nose, the size of your forehead, or your eyebrows, or your eyelashes, or your ears, or your hairline, your skin tone, your nostrils, your lips, your teeth, your chin, your boobs, your waist, your butt - I mean are you not exhausted yet? I'm exhausted for you! And this is what you've been handed. This is what you've been told you must do in order to even matter, in order for anyone to love you, in order to feel good about yourself. So I'll be the last guy to ever tell you this: **you're worth more than your body**. You're a human being and you deserve to be treated with dignity and respect.

G U Y S

Guys we do not need more low quality men in society. We

have enough of those do we not? I mean the world is as bad as it is because there's too many bad men running amok and not enough good men, like the ones reading this book, fully capable of standing up and doing something about it. What are you waiting for? A Captain America serum to be invented? An Iron Man suit to be invented? Are you waiting for an alien invasion where your video game skills are finally going to be useful in real life? It will never happen. I hate to break it to you. You're going to have to decide what kind of man you want to be or porn will decide it for you and I don't want to live in that future and that's why I wrote this book. The good news is greatness, **according to all of human history**, is something you just go out and take. I can point to great men and women all through history, to their portraits and paintings, and show you that they weren't very attractive or athletic, some didn't have great people skills, some were blind or deaf or disabled, but they still managed to do amazing things that history will forever remember. So what's your excuse?

CHAPTER 7

The Promise

Am my making any sense? No? Maybe? Look, whether you do what I did and you wait until you're married to have sex, or you do what my wife did, exploring sexually activity for a period in your youth only to realize how destructive it is and THEN wait, I can promise you one thing, as sure as the sun will rise tomorrow, you won't regret abstinence.

"Oh if only I hadn't been a virgin! My marriage would be so much better! If only I'd watched more porn! My life would be so much better! Sex with my spouse would be so much better!"

In all the years that I've been married to Gretchen, we've had a lot of fights, but I've never woken up next to that woman

and regretted my decision to abstain from sex until marriage
and spurn pornography, and I never will.

ABOUT THE AUTHOR

Jeromy Darling is a singer/songwriter, actor, speaker, mixed martial artist and advocate against sexual exploitation in all it's forms. He married his only girlfriend, Gretchen, on Sept. 1, 2002 and they're currently raising their 3 sons, Wyatt, Wilder and Wren, in Minnesota.